Farther From and Too Close to Home

Poems
by Gail Tremblay

Lone Willow Press
Omaha, NE

Also by Gail Tremblay

Talking to the Grandfathers (1981)
Indian Singing in Twentieth Century America (1990, rev. 1998)

Book design by: Lone Willow Press
Cover design by: Eric Hoffman

ISBN: ISBN-13: 978-1494446307 / ISBN-10: 1494446308

First Printing
Published by Lone Willow Press, P.O. Box 31647, Omaha, NE 68131

Dedication

This book is dedicated to so many friends, living and dead, who make and have made my life rich and bearable. I especially wish to remember Hisami Yoshida, Lillian Pitt, Joe Feddersen, Rick Bartow, Pauline Houx, Setsuko Tsutsumi, Therese Saliba, Tom Wright, Laurie Meeker, Maria Treviso, Ratna Roy, Fred Zydek, Bob Leverich, Marianne and Bud Bailey, Laura Grabhorn, Helen Klebesadel, Imna Arroyo, Angela Gilliam, Anne Fischel, Helen Thornton, Jorge Gilbert, Stan Shikuma, Tracy Lai, Alan Lau, Kazuko Nakane, Susan Platt, Cecilia Concepción Alvarez, Albert Smalls III, and Barbara Thomas. I also want to remember the spirits of Michio Teshima, Martha Tapia, Julie Bartow, Ernestine Kimbro, Angeline Nockai, Bruce Miller, Harry Fonseca, Marge Brown and my father whose presence in my life may no longer be physical, but whose memory is very important to me day after day. I want to thank the many very special students who have become my friends and co-conspirators on adventures. Finally, I want to dedicate this book to Jeffery Grice, M.D. who gave me the confidence to let him perform surgery on me when I had uterine cancer. His humanity and skill have given me rich years to write and make art, and for all the laughter and tears, and the fullness of my life over these years, I especially want to thank him.

Acknowledgments

The author wishes to acknowledge the following publications in which these poems were previously published:

"Owning Difference" in *Gone to Croatan: Origins of North American Dropout Culture* (Automedia/AK Press, 1993). "Owning Difference" and "An Onondaga trades with a woman who sings with a Mayan Tongue" in *Returning the Gift: Poetry and Prose from the First Native American Writers Festival* (The University of Arizona Press, 1994). "Surviving" in *Claiming the Spirit Within: A Sourcebook of Woman's Poetry* (The Nature Company, 1993). "Surviving" and "An Onondaga trades with a woman who sings with a Mayan tongue" in *CALYX Journal, Vol 17, no.1, 1993.* "In Praise of Flesh" and "To Travel Generations" in *Without Reservation: Indigenous Erotica* (Kegodonce Press, 2003). "Owning Difference," "An Onondaga trades with a woman who sings with a Mayan tongue," "Train Trip from Nogales to Mexico City, Day 2," "Rain Song," "In Homage to the Chinese Inventor who Invented "Gunpowder" without the Gun," "Surviving," and "Days" in *Indian Singing* (CALYX Books, 1998.) "Days" and "To Find a Tenderness" in *Raven Chronicles*, Vol 7, no 3, 1998. "*Casa de Cortez, Antigua, Veracruz*,""*En la casa museo de Augustin Lara, Veracruz,*" and "Seattle Aquarium, Spring, 1995" in *Raven Chronicles*, March, 1997.

Table of Contents

In the World Where I Find Myself

Too Close to Home

Possibilities for Being Human

Farther From Home
Mexico 1992 and 1995

Train Trip from Nogales to Mexico City: Day 2
(On first seeing *arboles de fuego* and other Southern things)

Flowers like trumpets of flame
greet the sun from treetops
in Sinaloa and Nayarit,
burn bright orange against dark
leaves that shine reflecting
all that gaiety back to the blue
arc of the sky. In the distance,
mountains and clouds touch
with intimate grace, the great stone
pillars and turrets above the trees
full of magic in the mist. Below,
workers wake to labor in rich
fields they do not own. In this land,
grandeur and suffering intermingle
so that beauty grows tender
amid layers of pain.

A few miles before we stop at Tepatitlan

Three horses gallop out of the dark
and run beside the train; they stretch
their necks and seem sleek and lean,
an apparition that reveals our speed.
The train begins to slow for the stop,
and, like magic, the horses veer away,
disappearing into the night. The moment
is like a startling dream; it vanishes
except for a lingering memory teaching
me how ephemeral reality can be.

Train Trip from Mexico City To Palenque: Day 7

Fog drifts over the backs of mountains
at dawn, as we travel between Cordoba
and Coatzalcoalcos, the train rocking us
into a steamy, gray day. We move past
towns with thatched houses, women hanging
out wash on fences surrounding yards
full of chickens and pigs and goats.
These towns are islands in a sea of rich fields
where pineapple and cane plants bristle,
leaves slicing the air as surely as workers
slice stalks to harvest sweetness
for a world too mean to value the magic
of those who wield the knives. Orchards make
landowners rich as the bananas, plantains, oranges,
mangoes, and papayas they export swell toward
a ripeness that excites the tongue's desires.
At every train stop, men and women come bearing
fresh food, singing out the names of their wares
and selling the wealth of the earth
so cheaply that one wonders how anyone
survives. The people on the train have
a moving feast as they travel to towns
to work and resume their lives. I travel,
careening toward new places so full
of contradiction that understanding becomes
the inevitable salt that spices tears.
Beauty, that bittersweet compassion,
is never enough in this world where greed
makes equality a concept the powerful most fear.

An Onondaga trades with a woman who sings with a Mayan tongue

We trade in Spanish, but you with the rich
cloth, tell your son how to behave in Mayan,
a language so beautiful it sings in my ears.
I watch him sit straight on the sofa in the hotel
lobby, your words giving dignity to his face.
I long to speak to someone in Onondaga, wondering
if you would recognize it as an indigenous tongue
since your world is so full of foreign languages,
and my people live so far north, our sounds
can not be familiar to your ears. Attracted
by my braids, you unwrap the fingerbraided,
tasseled band from your own and offer it for sale.
I feel hesitant because it is so outside
my own tradition, but in the end your insistence
and its beauty make it mine. I wish my Spanish
were better, so I could make you understand
why I may never wear it, but will always treasure
it because you were proud enough to keep the old ways
alive and to want to see my hair properly bound
according to your custom, making me less a stranger
in this, your sacred and most magic place.

Palenque

There are moments when genius becomes transparent
and shimmers in the mist; the monuments
it leaves are physical, rising solidly from plazas
surrounded by jungle, but the thought
that made form possible, that ephemeral
idea that marks history and organizes
human work merely whispers across centuries
so mystery remains intact. I sit on the bottom
step of the Temple of Inscriptions and watch
parrots dot the sky with yellow-green.
Everywhere the sound of water rushes
speaking of how this center nurtures life.
Macaws call and make explosions
of bright color as they move against leaves.
Generations ago their ancestors' feathers decorated
the heads of Mayan priests who prayed
in this place. Now plazas are green
with grass, and tourists yell in languages
the builders never heard. Their voices
cannot interrupt the grandeur defined
by an energy as palpable as rain feeding
earth, the jungle growing, the ruin
carved out in testimony to a brilliant past.

La mujer Maya

She weaves together the fabric of her society,
her work helping to make life possible
for her people. Tradition teaches her
to lean back, pulling the warp threads
straight so she can recreate the world
in patterns, some simple like the cloth
she wraps as skirts, others complex
like the patterns on the yokes of her shirts
that reveal which village her people
live in to those who know. She is expert
at raising threads so that animals prance
under rows of graceful birds. The weft thread
falls into place when she throws her shuttle;
things in her world become whole and beautiful.
It is this skill passed down from her mothers
that gives her these wares to market
on the streets in towns near ruins built
by her ancestors whose work attracts the world.
She trades her goods, and her children
eat. She enjoys the ironies; those ancients
whose genius created so much work
for the people, today help the people
to survive these hard times when they struggle
against those who steal their lands.
For generations, her people have understood
the complexity in patterns that move
the world in a song of days across
the mother, earth, who gives them life.
She works, knowing that song in a language
passed down so both tongue and fingers sing.

Rain Song

The rain falls gentle, a warm mist
as if the clouds sweat dew to feed
the sweet and turbulent Earth.
This moisture washes leaves
with yellow veins, long arching
palms, and all the lush growth
under trees I can not name
on this edge of the jungle.
Color explodes here; flowers
and birds bright against green
wake up the eye. Nothing dares
to be dull that can think
how to celebrate its life.
In a land so present
one can feel its breath, water
continues to make life possible.

Merida

In this colonizer's city, the sun caresses
palaces and churches built with stones
from Mayapan. Light dances on tiles,
fine veined marble mined in Italy
or France and bought with the blood
of Indians enslaved so the world
could have rope to tie things down.
In this colonizer's city, music fills
the streets. Women in *huipils* dance
like butterflies around men in white
cotton and beautifully woven straw
hats. Clarinets, guitars, and violins
played with sweet and sour notes
celebrate this *mestizo* world where the drum
beats out rhythms of a convoluted past.
What can't be denied or forgotten
is embroidered to make life beautiful.
Here, the rich attempt to buy grace, to enjoy
luxury, live the bittersweet life that isolates
them from the poverty they create.
They practice ignorance and never focus
on the beggars in the street who reach
with cupped hands for heavy coins
where the serpent dangles in the jaws
of the eagle. In this gracious,
colonizer's city where lovers meet
and life unravels too many mysteries,
in the palace of government, the great
painter, Pacheco, recorded the history
of men made of corn who struggled
to stay free. His vision keeps amnesia away.

Finding Uxmal

Wrong turns, circuitous journeys can be revelations.
We came on a one-lane road that wound seductively
between stands of tall grass intergrown with flowers,
bright dots of yellow that were touched by mouths
of butterflies beneath a blue sky where the sun
blessed everything alive. There was no distance
visible, and the world hummed with insects
as it spun through space. Occasionally solitude
would be broken by Mayan men bicycling home
bearing loads of firewood on their backs. Then,
suddenly, we were born into a village
of thatched houses where people worked in close
relationship with earth. They were intimate,
supported life, knew how to build a world
from scratch so it moved in harmony with place.
Corn, beans and chilies grew while turkeys
gawked around the yards, their feathers ruffling
in the wind revealing skin on thin necks
above plump bodies; the birds were almost comical.
People moved with grace and were shy
in Mayan when we asked directions. Full
of energy, this world was rich in tastes
and smells, sounds; it echoed with people
keeping a gracious way of life alive.

In a few miles we found Muna,
the main road, distant horizons
that allowed us to see the landscape
laid out like a rolling forest
between fields. Then we found the ruin,
a white skeleton of stones in high country.
We climbed its steps and felt awe looking
into the carved faces of the gods.
The glyphs written by ancient hands
spoke a mute language across centuries.
This center spoke of pomp and majesty,

the movement of ceremony and sacrifice
across days that marked long cycles
of gain and loss. It spoke of water,
that treasure, rain flowing to a hungry
Earth, the weeping sky, a spiritual force
that made men willing to die to dwell
with Gods. These buildings were raised
above plazas in a scared geometry so beauty
could make suffering bearable awhile.
But a carved row of thatched houses on a wall
reminded us that continuity keeps things
meaningful alive. What does not support life
is abandoned, no matter how graceful to the eye.

Listening to Voices at Chichen Itza
    (Two Ways of Seeing)

So many spirits haunt this place where divinity
dwelled in men who transformed nature by sacrificing
themselves according to a star struck design
that swept in with a plumed serpent from Tula,
Venus waking before dawn to shine on thousands
of images of Kulkulcan. Only the most gifted
were fit for such a holy death, the captains
who with agility used shoulders, heads, or legs
to send the ball flying through a ring in the sacred
game. They, the most magical, careless of mortal life,
could play while thousands watched knowing the stakes
were a swift stab with an obsidian knife, a stroke
that freed the heart from earthly desires and filled
the wells that fed the city. These knew no fear of death
and mystify the modern mind, hungry for life at any cost,
distracted by the passion for ordinary pleasures. Awed
by the grandeur, foreigners murmur asking awkward
questions in a Babel of languages, seldom grasping
the real meaning of the answers. Not sons or daughters
of the gods, these citizens of the world can not imagine
bringing salvation to a people in need of rain to feed
the thirsty corn that has sustained generations
and made life possible. Worried there is no resurrection,
they shudder, preferring to be saved than to be savior.
To them the elegant sport that ends death is torture.

Casa de Cortez, Antigua Veracruz

Light sifts through leaves of trees
that perch atop the walls of this ruin
and send adventitious roots scaling down
to finger dirt beneath red tiled floors
and round stones that pave the patio
of this old house, first skeletal remains
of a colonial floor plan laid out
to make foreigners feel at home
in someone else's country. One wonders
at Cortéz's luck, given as a gift Malintzin.
At first, he tried to give her away
to one of his lieutenants, but realized
it didn't matter whether or not
he found her pretty—she was his fate;
she had the tongue he would use
to reshape a continent, to make allies
he would later betray as he did her.
But at this point in the story,
it was her skill with languages
that amazed him— in a mere month,
she could whisper in his ear words
he learned from his mother; she could
answer his million questions, name
the unnamable things he had never seen.
He was her passage out of slavery;
she, a *Mexica* noblewoman, hurt
at being tossed away by her own family.
In this house, she became mistress,
gave orders, advised the conqueror.
It was here that she learned
about a god whose death would end
the need to sacrifice to the sun,
and in whose name millions
would be sacrificed to foreign greed.
One wonders what she understood
of her role in history as she learned

to eat his bread. When she was baptized
Doña Marina, did she ever guess
how much suffering she would help
initiate? The people re-christened her
La Malinche, she whose spirit haunts
these shadows trapped by her ancient
desires to have things the world refused,
getting instead an endless notoriety—
who by aiding the abuser became also abused.

En la casa museo de Augustin Lara, Veracruz
       (For Lidia Huante)

           I wandered around looking at pictures,
           photos that measured a lifetime spent
           writing the music beautiful women loved
           and sang, women who teased lyrics alive
           with their tongues, making notes caress
           like kisses 'til a whole generation swooned
           over this man's words, rhythms, his harmonies
           that vibrated so gracefully against the skin.
           And the women in the photos were not just
           beautiful, they sang insouciantly, the spice
           of their spirits lit their voices, they gave
           more light than candles— they were the saints
           every sinner wished to pray to. The house sat
           on a corner, a pristine white and full of wind
           blowing in over a shimmering sea. Everything
           felt fresh and full of whispering energy.
           The piano was placed near a window
           overlooking the waves, home of conches
           and luminous fish, a place where palm trees
           couldn't help but get a little drunk on the sun.
           I sat on the white divan, and a charming
           older man played every song I named.
           Twice I cried, longing for you, my friend,
           whose mother, a cook for farm workers,
           died much too young when you were only
           seventeen. We who grew up on different
           coasts, on rock and roll, years later
           would celebrate your mother's memory
           cooking molé for Thanksgiving and playing
           Toña La Negra singing with that weighty
           woman's voice all these marvelous
           compositions that keep memory alive—
           Oh how I miss your presence in this room.

China, 1995 and 1999

In Homage to the Chinese Inventor who Invented
    "Gunpowder" without the Gun

Fire works its way across the sky
more subtly than lightning, stitches
burning scraps into cascades of sparks,
explodes into spheres of color expanding
out and creating chrysanthemums of light
and smoke that make the dark suddenly
dimensional and full of rowdy voice
declaring man has invaded space
and sending tiny rockets spiraling
above the earth to celebrate
the transitory nature of a flickering
art whose birth is its destruction.

Shanghai

Renewal— the old walled city, marked
only by its Lion Gate, attempts to recreate
a century gone by, to give itself a grandeur
only the rich possessed. Workers rebuild arching
slate and tile roofs supported by graceful ribs
of polished wood. Longing for a country life,
roof peaks are ornamented with carved
pigs and roosters, but the phoenix rising
above them all proclaims ancient legends
are too graceful to fail to rule this roost.
Below, amid dozens of small shops, crowds
of people everywhere smile and nod,
and sometimes stare, watching tourists
staring back— in the center of this city
made of many cities, of new neighborhoods
sprouting up while next door people struggle
to live in worn houses about to collapse—
here, where change grows more quickly
than plums or rice, one finds history
revised and gussied up to please the eye.

Lake Li, Wuxi

The morning is mysterious and gray,
fog making the mountains distant,
the horizon as indistinct as breath
against the wind. This blurring of edges
focuses attention on what is close:
the subtle changes of color and texture
in the trees, the dark pine against red
roof tiles in the park, the motion
of dragonflies, wings a delicate veined
cellophane slicing air with hardly
a sound. The five-storied pagoda, framed
with bamboo scaffolding, becomes a work
in progress, a place for builders to practice
ancient arts so the past takes on new life.
Work takes place surrounded by the whirring
of cicadas, the whirring of boat engines
moving goods and tourists. The water
ripples into shore, caresses edges
of land as gently as the general, after whom
the lake is named, caressed the woman
of incomparable beauty he carried to this place.
Looking back across the centuries, lovers remember
and, touching, keep the passions of the past alive.

West Lake, Hangzhou

By day, light shimmers in ripples on the surface;
sun's reflected fire tempts butterflies to wander
over water, circle one another like the souls
of haunted lovers hunting for the magic place
where love was hardly possible near lotus pools
where flowers nodded above wavering green leaves,
their dance a gentle leaning into intimate warm
breezes, steamy air teasing buds to unfold,
to bloom and fade away. Conjuring a different history
where girls can get their way, young lovers, guarded
by mountains, sit by the shore, watching dragonflies,
as startling as sticks of coral with wings, dart about,
perch on broken lotus stalks red against the green.
Lovers move their heads together, whisper and dream
of magic nights where touch can heal a weary
heart. These lovers wait 'til everything is dark.
The lake becomes a mirror's mirror, reflects the moon
moving across heavens and mirroring the sun. Moon fills
three pools on an island with light and makes lit
windows in skyscrapers on the eastern shore seem
more distant than the stars. Fingers search for ways
to learn the name hidden in moon's most pregnant dreams.

Xian

Flying west across China, land
of impressive mountains and mighty
rivers that feed fertile valleys,
it is startling to recognize the familiar
geography of cornfields, sunflowers, potatoes,
and watermelons amid the pomegranate groves,
an incredible patchwork on this earth
surrounding the old walled city whose tower
roofs arch gracefully toward hazy blue skies.
In this ancient place, cradle of Han culture
at the head of Silk Road, the first emperor
built a clay army to guard his corpse
from rebellious farmers. Undaunted, they burned
his tomb, but their descendants have taken
centuries to overthrow the tyrannies he dreamed
into being. Here indigenous, American plants
poke their hardy roots into ground
that welcomes them— are tended by caring,
dark-haired growers who look familiar,
who, like relatives, save their seeds so that, season
after season, these plants can come to feed the people
in this nation working hard to find ways
to help human beings survive harsh winds.

In the Garden behind the Gate to Heaven, Forbidden City, Beijing

In this walled garden, thousands of beautiful women
were kept to please the eye of one imperious man.
Most sighed, learned to live with melancholy.
Wrapped in silken threads, they composed lonely songs
and watched while a few were caressed, grew round
with child, played with tiny fingers, sucked on toes
and knew the pressure of small, pink mouths sucking
at their tender breasts. At night, alone, women dreamt
of the only man allowed to notice, to nod at them
at parties where revelers climbed the inner stair
of the Mountain of Piled Excellence to view the moon.
These women longed for the one man most women
knew would never grace their rooms. Living in a world
where hunger for tender hands haunted lives like pale
ghosts— where women were too numerous
to all find love— only the rarest found out that the magic
of a lover's touch could make her bloom like a blushing
peony unfolding to release a burst of golden stamens
hidden in the center of soft, ruffled petals. Sad women
passed their springs away, grew old in the company
of jealous girls who lost all hope and turned from grace
because only the most favored would be chosen
by a solitary emperor who remembered perhaps
a hundred names on a list too long for any man to know.

Years later, after revolution opened the Gate to Heaven,
graceful women dressed in their best, traveled miles
across China to sip tea with husbands in what were once
forbidden pavilions and to dream this love was possible
and theirs alone. Couples leaned together, held hands,
looked past their feet and smiled at flowers formed
by colored stones embedded in the surface of the path.
Turning corners, they startled sculptures of fantastic,
gilded beasts, and nodded shyly at young lovers
whose bright eyes swallowed one another's bodies
in a glance. People watched as hands reached to discover

those of a partner on a railing, as shoulders touched,
as men and women whispered sweet, simple words
and laughed. Pairs of eyes followed the gnarled branches
of ancient trees that have stood for centuries inside these walls
and seen so many seasons come and go. Eyes climbed past leaves
to study a sky framed by towers that used to guard this microcosm
of the world. Here, where lotus flowers bloom in a marble pool
and rocks are piled to create the illusion of mountains
rising from a plain, where everything is circumscribed
and planned with artful grace, it is pleasure to share
artifice together and to know after a few sweet hours
a couple can choose to escape together out the garden gate.

Precipitous Mountains

We fly into Guilin stretching to see
the Li River winding like a luminous
ribbon between precipitous mountains
that rise like gigantic boulders from this flood
plain toward the sky. Washed clean
by some receding primeval ocean
that haunts human imagination
with a reality more ephemeral than we long
to know— immense rocks stand exposed
and naked in the land. Once on the ground,
the journey into town reveals the scale—
we move like scholars in an ancient landscape,
dwarfed by nature, small among shadows
which grow as sun moves closer
to the horizon on this planet whirling
us and mountains through space toward a darker
heaven punctuated by stars. We wonder,
if in the morning, after a whole night of turning,
mist will whisper among bamboo
in valleys between the folds of these eminent
stones, and if we will wake to scenes
like those in scrolls we saw on the walls of distant
museums— scenes caught by skillful painters
trapping some transitory moment from centuries
ago that will permit us the comforting illusion
that life on earth is constant and secure.

In the World Where I Find Myself

For Poets whose Work Sustains Me
(For Lucille Clifton, Linda Hogan, June Jordan,
Joy Harjo, Audre Lorde, Liz Woody and too many people to name)

The work of the poet is to comfort the afflicted
and afflict the comfortable.

Judson Jerome

You who see pain everywhere,
who may meet pain on any street corner
rocking out of the sweet walking dark
alley into your life, you who
witness the hungry growing frail,
the twelve year old boy thrown in jail
for stealing food
in a country where a mountain of food
becomes sweet, sticky waste everyday—
you who cry for the children beaten,
bruised and broken by adults who lose
patience with the desperation
in their lives and forget to love,
you who watch the women afraid to walk
alone, shivering in the dark trying
to get home without having to strike back
at those who would attack anyone who dares
to be vulnerable or tender or strong
enough to care in a world warped
by those who desire power over
as a way to feel in charge,
you who mourn for men and women broken
by work that makes them weak, that kills
the will to think and pays too little
to allow for joy or play or growing
ways to celebrate a life,
you who listen to earth moaning
from the strain of being stripped
and poisoned so the greedy can grow rich
while life becomes more tenuous

as the fragile web unravels, and the hole
in the sky makes the sky that has
sustained life dangerous, so existence
grows more cancerous, loss more commonplace,
you who complain that torture and bombs
are no solution and can never make earth
a safer place for those that suffer,
you who sing about sorrow and cradle
the weary souls that dream love
and bread are possible— in a world
that breaks my heart, it is you who make
me less lonely, it is your work
that helps to set me free.

The Metaphysics of Homelessness: Reflections on the U.S. Economy

"Spare change, spare change," as if there ever
could be such a thing in this stingy world
where everyone needs too much, especially
the rich. The generous move out of step, giving
too little to mend another life. He stands before
me, ragged, leaning on his crutch, complaining his
leg hurts, that he is a nickel short of the price
of a room. I only have a dollar with me, glad
to part with it knowing the pleasure of a room
of one's own, how even a strange bed can become
home in a private place where one can shut out
strangers or invite a friend. He is too grateful,
calls me sister, moves the braid on my shoulder
and wakes my loneliness. I tell him it is nothing,
knowing that's not true, trying to be respectful
in a world where I have not figured out how
to make things equal and still survive. This is
no labor of love, having to face a system
that promotes hunger, kills those that try
to dismantle it: this is no labor of love.
Inside, a chasm of sorrow fills with the relentless
murmuring of those whose need is more acute
than my ability to give. Inside, I hone my anger;
my tongue grows sharp; I long to cleave the air
with my voice. I make my friends uneasy talking
of these things. I want to know how it is possible
to be good when we do not organize to make change.
I want to know how much suffering we can bear to watch
before we must choose between suffering and action.
On this planet, none of us is alone.

Family Values
(One strategy for avoiding loss)

In the 60s, society still wanted to closet
girls away— to hide the evidence
young men could penetrate the dark
secret folds of a virgin's desire to feel
wanted in a lonely world. A need for illusion
drove girls into homes for unwed mothers
from which they emerged shaken and alone,
trapped by needing to pretend that nothing
had transformed their innocent bodies
into vessels that could contain so much
sorrow. These young women were haunted
by visions of distant cities where strangers cooed
over the babies real mothers could never recognize
as their own. At home, the girls barely dared
to cry for fear others would know. Only
a few lucky rebels escaped convention—
gave in to their own complicated need
to nurture creatures fed by every breath
they took over nine months of yearning
while bellies swelled, and skin grew as taut
and hard as watermelons. Inside, cells divided,
sweet flesh transforming itself into a being
so miraculous that magic made it inevitably
theirs. In the end, shame became irrelevant.
They took their babies home to a world not yet
ready to enjoy the fruit that teenage desire
to know passion had made possible— and
sometimes love let everybody grow a bit more kind.

Strategies to Survive Living in American Towns

During those days when sorrow is so deep
it takes too much energy to cry, one rocks
silence inside a body cavity where nothing
seems empty of grief. In a world where kindness
seems powerless against cruelty, torturers
can inhabit any home on your block, and the lives
of children can be disfigured by adults who forget
that love is not about bending others to do
unspeakable tasks to feed an unbearable need
to know power. On days when friends, knocking
on the door, shiver in terror, clothes torn
because someone has jumped out of the alley
and grabbed and grabbed and grabbed with greedy
hands at a body that is not his, it becomes
an endless struggle to find the words to comfort
where nothing is comfortable. One wonders
how sunrises and flowers usher in new days,
and seasons grace experience again while men
plot to exploit this graceful planet that makes
life possible. The contradictions overwhelm
the sense of what is natural, what is familiar
inside the sacred circle where magic is a way
of finding harmony and balance, and power
is the will to give and serve, to support life
in all its mystery. It is true, that even
among indigenous people, confusion and selfishness
were always a possibility; tragedy could always
make someone envy those that did not suffer as much
until the beaten longed to take things they did not
have. But a whole culture that sings about scarcity,
embraces hunger, that grows so insatiable thousands
forget to share the wild fruits that the dirt
in its profound fertility provides to feed
the multitudes, and instead destroys these things
that make survival real, such confusion maims
and replicates the dulling anguish that kills

feeling. In such a world tears are worth
the struggle to keep care alive, and giving
is the only way to establish new patterns that will
tell the heart that hurt is not inevitable.

Reflections on Manifest Destiny

Only in those bright moments
when the hunger to shut
the dear, dark world away
is made manifest by the tortured
bodies of those who love the land—
only then is it clear that the destiny
at work is the destruction
of the nurturing Earth
by those whose vision
makes them meditate on the end.
The rest of us, not working
to create some inevitable apocalypse,
mourn and count the days.
No millennium looms on our ancient
calendars; time rocks us
in other dreams, moon and stars
marking the moment to plant
or the weeks to hold the ceremonies
that thank each growing thing
which roots itself or moves
across the planet in its own special
pattern. There are a million
things we choose not to create.
Amid the chaos, we try to remember
balance, that simple dance
that moves lightly, takes little
space, that celebrates the possibility
for breath. We know the conquerors'
fascination when they fondle death;
we've seen them strip the dirt
off bones, caress grave goods,
display remains, as surely as we've seen
them profit from sweet
fruit they tear from trees. They rape
the ground to manufacture impossible
dreams. Glittering nightmares grow

up around us; each year more guns
and bombs increase the terror.
We know the path "from sea
to shining sea" was never long
enough, and now the surface
of the water hides great, garbage
dumps where poison leaks, a steady
drip so soundless, death whispers
as it kills. In large cities, air
suffocates as particles hang visible,
glowing in the sun. Confusion dances
in this buzzing light trying to distract
us, to make us believe that power lives
in their desperate vision. Still,
in many nations, there are those
who cherish what makes life possible.
Some prepare to gather where the world
will start again, many wait for new
revelation that will lay to rest
the memory of a tortured god
who found returning to his torturers
was more than he could bear.

Jan. 16 1991: War begins

Again, children are dying,
blood staining the ground,
buildings burning, collapsing,
breaking tender bodies, this time
in Baghdad— fabled city
on the Tigris whose modern buildings
are rooted in an ancient world
that has sunk in layers
under sand and been built
several times anew. All I can feel
is sorrow at this destruction;
all the sweet and tender lives
that will not flower on this edge
of the desert. Soon sweet and tender
relatives who traveled from my own country
will die when the battles
after this bombing begin. So much to loose
because leaders do not love peace,
do not love life, give in to greed.
revel in their own power by creating
death that ends in bones bleaching
among rubble on the sand. So much ends
in body bags full of dead meat
that once inspired love and now
will fill families with years of grief.
The keening cries
of mothers have just begun
on two continents. The fragile web that holds
creation unravels. We who wish
to be peacemakers, to weave the world—
to knit things whole again
must go to work to mend the fabric
of an earth torn to shreds
by those who are not brave
enough to love their enemies,
to build a world of friends.

Seattle Aquarium, Spring, 1994

Undulating, sinuous, as though fins
were wings and the underwater circling
outside the glass dome were a dark
kind of flight where muted light
reflected iridescent off scales,
illuminated edges of eyelids and gills,
glowed 'til it haunted the dreams
of those who must suck air into lungs.
Staring out from this underwater room,
we watch a world not our own
where things resonate to the rhythm
of tides and wind whispering its name
on the surface in waves less constant
than a wish. If we lived on a planet
without crimes that result in reports
of testimony by Argentine lieutenants
about large, dark fish following
planes bearing the disappearing
dead out to sea for a feast
and never learned of nature's bleak
need to devour loved ones
that would otherwise rot
and pollute miraculous deep
canyons hidden in the pocket of ocean,
this sweet interlude below the watery
surface of Puget Sound might feel,
for a moment, magically benign.

In This World

We who desire song, cannot sing
just for the sake of singing.
This moment seems so sad it eats our tongues;
our words dance deformed by too much
moaning. Laugher rattles in our ears
and leaves us unnerved on uneven streets
where the tortured keep stumbling
across their torturers. Terror dries up
too many tears when children must
learn to commit crimes to feed mothers
who are condemned by economy
and policy, are sentenced
to the horrors of poverty. Hunger hums
more relentlessly than the flies that infest
the world of the starving; it drones
drowning out sweet music so nothing
can lull us on this prickly planet
where groups of ruthless fools create
the illusion that greed is the only road
to a beautiful life of graceful things
which can insulate ugly souls from themselves.
Searching for a more resonant song,
together, we must learn to improvise
on instruments that mean to transform human
consciousness of what is right and good.

Unraveling Cruelty

Sometimes I wake; there is so much
wanting in me, hunger, an insatiable
dance rocking more need than could ever
make sense. No taste or touch or intimate
explosion between my legs could fill
the empty well of my being. I stare
into space and shiver before the hollow
throats of thousands starving on an earth
parched by too much pillaging. I long for
clean rain, for living water not killed
by chemicals, to wash all this sorrow away,
to quench the thirst of this circling planet
so that every creature could drink
the titillating nectar that makes life possible.
It worries me that so much of human work
has become an irrational act done without
thought to profit a few. So many of those
who nurture the land are hunted, rounded up,
punished for daring to remember how to love,
how to maintain ancient relationships
between themselves and other beings who allow
community to live in balance. I fear
those that don't recognize the sacredness
in plants, who create deserts, mowing trees
so ancient that their knowing has sheltered
generations of lovers from hundreds
of species. So often, I see my own complicity,
my inability to simplify my life in holy ways
that will free us from this galloping plunge
toward oblivion. I long to give an image,
to sing a rich, convoluted song that vibrates
until knowing is born, until we learn the thing
we need will entail a patient unraveling
of this cruelty some think is human nature.

In Hope of Peace
        September 11–October 11, 2001

        Death flies in on silver wings,
        flies in through walls and windows—
        flies in and in, explodes in flames,
        taking its messengers with it—
        snatching them amid dark prayers—
        snatching thousands in mid-sentence,
        amid their work, things scattering,
        going up in smoke, falling, falling—
        rubble falling away from skeletons
        of molten steel, burying ash, teeth,
        fractured bits of flesh and bone, burying
        so much hope and human wish
        between sunrise and mid-day.

        And then the aftermath begins—
        not that anything surprises me
        in this world where sorrow wears
        at millions, and daily, children die
        for want of food and clear, clean water.
        For years, I have had to negotiate
        with grief because borders never make
        me blind to the pain of others sharing
        space on this small, suffering planet
        rushing in a spiral after the sun
        in search of light— too little light.
        Speeches and votes condoning war
        make me wild with worry; why
        are there never enough blessings
        to create a world without terror. Shame
        wells in me, pools near my heart;
        my taxes pay for so much cruelty—
        too little love, too little generosity.

Since Sunday, October 7th, the sound
of bombs has haunted my dreams—
doubled my grief— I long for compassionate
courts, trials, evidence — for infinite justice
instead of more dark death— for life
sentences to do good works until God
forgives all the terrorists who forget to love
the creatures on this sweet, revolving earth.

Half Way Around the World

In this season of rainbows when rain
and sun mix to make color arc
against the sky, when a million shoots
put up leaves and buds, and flowers
open to drink the damp in the welcoming
turning of the planet that brings spring,
why does melancholy come to haunt
my days? Each day is getting longer, lit
by an incandescent ball of fire we follow
through space riding on the back of a rowdy
orb of earth whose inconsistent love
still gives us life. At such a moment,
I should know joy, should celebrate surviving
another interminable winter of short, dark days.
In this land where hyacinths give off heady
perfume, where plum and cherry blossoms
begin to fill the air with sweet, subtle scents,
and tulips start to take on a riot of color
against the ground, spirits should lift.
But each morning, the news of distant bombs
and guns, the death tolls in the desert, of children
dying in the fertile crescent between the Tigris
and Euphrates, of young soldiers from three
countries killing one another on the edge of cities,
attacking and defending a scrap of dirt that covers
rich underground pools of oil; each morning brings
disquieting shame which beats in my body
like the echoing sounds of munitions hitting
the walls of buildings in some far country.
I can not bear to fund, with money taken
each month from my salary, this terrible
destruction of place and fragile flesh
that like my own could love to tend a garden,
to grow a grove of fruit producing trees.
How can I, made guilty of this crime by leaders
I would never choose, ever do enough

when in the midst of a shimmering spring
I have not been able to stop the flow of blood,
to heal the terrible wounds that stop the hearts
of those I only wish to love in this small world
where the flowers in my yard become a sad memorial
for too many graves, half way around the world.

Too Close to Home

Uncommon Vision

Since I was a child, I have lived in a world
where the bears browse along the edges of high
fields full of new berries looking for the magic
ripeness to sweeten their tongues. Sun warms
dark fur and creates great bear-shaped shadows
that lumber across the ground. Sitting quiet
upwind, I have always longed for a different world,
wondered an impossible intimacy, wondered if
I gently nibbled an ear, would the miraculous
thick fur cover my teeth on both sides. Even
in dreams, it is a question I dare not answer.
All my life I have harbored this impossible love
for things I must leave the world of men
to discover. I have walked away from the edges
of towns, walked away from the other women
tending the corn, and climbed the dark trails
under trees looking for impossible romance
where no language penetrates— where one can
merely caress with longing eyes the things
it is too dangerous to touch. In those places
I have waited for uncertain revelation, have
learned the miraculous calm that comes when one
sits patiently unraveling expectation. I have
teased the edges of that common knowing that
vibrates in the light between living things
who work in different ways to make being possible.
And when I have returned to the whirling reality
humans in this century have created for themselves,
it makes so little sense, I have had to disagree.

Owning Difference

Strangers sense difference, stare,
try to define the unacceptable trait,
the dusky gene that explains what is so
disturbing about the cut of an eye, the length
of an earlobe, the flatness at the back of a head.
The kindest adjective they find is exotic.
At least once a month someone looking
for an explanation asks, "What are you anyway?"
The answer, "Human," denies too much,
the sweet embrace of one's parents, dark
and light, the mixing of eternal forces
across boundaries. How can one explain
complex migrations, the chemistry of passion,
the ability to risk ostracism that make
this life possible. I own difference
not because I chose it, but because love
made it inevitable. I grew conscious, knowing
life was full of contradictions, knowing
the stately dance around the drum was a gift
I earned caressing earth with every step. Refusing
to vanish, I can only answer with my dark name.

Sweet Mirage

In intimate moments when even light
was full of grace and fell gently
on contours softening the hard edges
of reality, his touch woke tremors
and filled that empty place where blood
washes possibility away. Love became
a net woven of moments when the fingers
searched the hidden fabric in the folds
of skin, a net that held passion
when, like a tight-rope walker, it lunged
from its solitary perch to haunt my conscious
mind. For hours at a time, I lost
the familiar loneliness and learned
to trust another being would surround
me with his arms if I looked with asking
eyes and touched my upper lip
with the flicking tip of my tongue.
Nuance overshadowed meaning and the careening
sensation made so much seem possible.
I dreamed of an eternity of days,
of generations that would bear the mark
of our bodies wound together in the spiral
staircase that defined their cells.
I planned to braid the hair of grandchildren,
teaching them the prayer that binds the people,
and giving the singular names of ancestors
as gifts to guide them to a useful life.
For a few months, I nurtured wishes, rocking
them in the cradle of my arms, forgetting
the transitory nature of things built
on desire. When violence came, I was not
ready to bear its cruelty; his death killed
all my pretty fantasies, and I was left
to explore the dark and learn alone
the price of surviving a life created
by the sweet mirage that longing makes.

I sat still with memory and held
on to the edge of a vulnerable world
where choosing meant uncertainty. I took
the risk and pain embroidered touch
with subtle marks that shape my sense;
I cannot wait for things that cannot be.

Merely a Gift
(To a younger poet)

All I have done is not refuse;
I allowed you into the place
I inhabit when you could not choose
to go. You came bringing your pain
and filling my life with cares,
a web that glistens in the light,
collects dew, and traps me in ways
you'll never know. The distance
between us stretches, and when you choose,
I will be alone. For me, desire is forbidden;
it only hastens loss, but I have learned
to embrace life with all its thorns,
to drink in the beauty with every sense.
The dark that waits can never catch
me unaware; infinite space is haunted
by the stars. I have no need to be
a center; love is merely a gift one gives
away, a seed one plants and nurtures
so, with luck, the world will be beautiful
and rich. It is ephemeral and can't be held.
Take what you will; many streams fill my well.

Finding What's Accessible

Waking to the dark dream my life has become,
to uncertainty haunting pathways in my spine,
I sink into a body that resists my will to move.
I adjust legs as heavy as bags of sand; in air,
they are no more than ballast to keep my torso
tied to earth. I desire flight, desire to sink
into a watery world where legs will float free,
so I can cross space as easily as a seal. I long
for the impossible grace of a fish leaping in spray,
that restless motion that breaks past familiar
elements and wakes strange sensation at the edge
of what we know. Too old to grow gills and fins,
I learn to sit on a wheeled throne and scheme
to get things done. I refuse to give in to sweet
despair, to allow this loss of cells that stops
the electric flow that once led me to dance,
to kill my will to go. Choosing, I touch things
close and dear, dare to accept the sweet caresses
of those brave enough to care. My world rolls
between obstacles, eyes touching what I no longer
reach, making memory reel in the textures— mud
pressing against the arches of feet as the undertow
carries dreams of the world I used to inhabit
out to sea. I long for moments filled with whispers
that flutter in puffs of breath against my ear,
for the exchange of secrets that reveal the raw
wound that experience can become. I learn lessons
only stillness can teach, explore the bittersweet
magic of constant motion, riding this planet
that revolves around a star that consumes itself
to make life with all its contradictions possible.
Unable to walk the field, I accept that pleasure
spins in a web of spokes traveling this hard road.

Echoes: Quinault Beach, 1992

Drunk on sun and the sound of surf, I sit,
prisoner, trapped on a stump watching friends
who can walk run barefoot at the border of an ocean
whose waves daily rearrange the edges of dirt
where land becomes sand kissed with too much salt.
These moments— when life is so full that joy
and the pain of loss mix to become sensation tingling
in the wind, touching things only the eye or heart
can reach— these very moments grow into an elegant
torture where limitation and possibility become
strands interwoven in a fabric so strange
one learns to appreciate the beauty of one's own
deformity. Down the beach small pines gnarled
by the wind grow, rooted in rocks that are islands
at high tide. These islands are marooned now, waiting
for the waves to wash their feet. I watch as birds whirl
and reach for branches as wild and barren as driftwood
growing from the bases of uprooted trees. This raw
touch of claw and wood rattles my sense and awakes
dead feeling so that the moan in my gut escapes
to my throat. I murmur alone, rocking a song,
listening to the wind blown sand make a hollow
sound that echoes feelings I dare not speak.

Nothing to Give

The woman was young, blonde, beautiful
like the girls in slick magazines who model
jeans. She chose to wear a bone choker
with an ermine tail as though it is possible
to appropriate a culture by wearing its artifacts.
She read a poem in which she said that she was
the white girl who always wanted to be Indian
when she grew up. I sat feeling sick, recognizing
that strange phantom pain in the gut, listening
to her romantic distortions about Eagle Boy dancing
in her dreams, about cruel Indian men who undressed
her and then scolded her for being naked before
them when she was on her moon. She invented
unreality because she refused to witness the real
hard work of living in a world distorted by forced
assimilation, by faked authenticity, by loss
that beat in counter rhythm near the heart
and made the whole world seem out of balance.
She did not speak of struggle, stolen land,
the Earth raped so that strangers could reap
great profits no matter what the cost. Her desire
was for vision to fill an empty life. One more
taker, she invented ceremonies that mystified,
that made healing seem a hollow exercise untied
from the web of light that weaves things seamlessly
into being, untied from the people who for generations
shared a sense of what made things whole in a given
place. I sat and watched speechless, caught,
too paralyzed to walk away and make a scene,
aware how often revelation is impossible to explain.

Diversity
        (For K.F.)

While I point, my friend cuts daffodils,
reminisces about going to the gardens
at Virginia Woolf's old estate in England
in the spring, about thousands of blooms
that mark for him the beginning of new
seasons and the melancholy passing of old
love. For me, these flowers have fewer
complications, no associations with past
relationships. They stand simple and fragrant
along the edges of my garden, their golden
stamens thick with pollen in the center
of flaring cups surrounded by a circle
of pale, graceful petals, almost chaste
in this cool weather before the heavy bees
fly buzzing from flower to flower. I take
five blossoms to my kitchen, cut and burn
the stems, arrange them so they stand,
a spare arrowhead of yellow amid arching leaves
rising from a flat Chinese bowl. I set them
on my counter beneath a hand-colored photograph
of Tatanka Iyotanka, the one called Sitting Bull,
who had visions and seven wives until he was
murdered fifty-five years before my birthday
to the day. My friend talks of his present
wife, her desire to grow things, of the obstacles
to planting and planning for a future in this
uncertain world. I revel in the turning, the slow
and gentle warming of earth rotating toward the sun
and marvel at how lives shared in the same town
can work out such different ways to see and be.

Surviving

I dream of dancing naked under stars,
the dew on grass dampening my ankles,
the moon, sensuous ancestor, calling
to my blood. I dream the impossible
moment when tongues touch, try to forget
how much I've lost. In these dark
moments, sensation wakes like an ancient
hunger that will never be satisfied. Nothing
insulates me from memory. The fire that fills
me with electric pulse, that makes my meat
long for that strange animal heat it once
possessed, desires even now when this graceless
body moves in fits and starts. It is difficult
to forget the pleasure of running, the quick
pulse feeding my whole being so even skin
seemed too small, my breath rushing past ears
to meet wind in my hair. Now there is no speed,
only the struggle of muscle working to cross
space, the deliberate choice to survive pain,
and the will to remember love is inescapable.

Letter Poem Chasing Richard Hugo's Ghost

Dear Richard,
    When we met, I was already past thirty,
    fat, would never be a beauty again
    although I still could dance circles
    around most women half my age
    and make a passionate metaphor
    when I was in the mood. I was
    no longer interested in taking men
    as lovers. You were bald, portly,
    smoked too much, limped gracefully
    and had already begun to cough, but talked
    the most elegant stories, and when you read
    poems, I wept at the way you teased
    honesty from such simple words.
    You struggled so with being human,
    learning to forgive yourself for failing
    to fit and fitting all too well in that white
    male world where one was taught
    to suppress feeling and dog eat dog
    and dose yourself with drink when pain
    rose up inevitable. Your incredible
    tenderness, which you could never fight
    or drink away, burned in your words
    as you fenced with expectation and lost
    as many duels as you won. After your reading,
    when you read my poems, it mattered
    too much when you enjoyed the way
    my language sang. In that moment
    you taught me how to write a long
    line so it would never sag and touched
    my shoulder and asked me to write
    and send you poems as new ones came
    staggering in from the dark. A few months
    later, I heard that you had been diagnosed
    with cancer— no surprise. My poems
    continued to stagger out, thick blocks

of words I could never address to you,
but wherever your ghost dances,
I want you to know you taught me well.

Yours,
Gail

Letter Poem to Fred Zydek Who Lives Miles
   ·   from the Edge of the Continent

Dear Fred,
     How can it be your 60th "year to heaven,"
     or for that matter my 52nd, each of us
     waking so many mornings to court
     song, caught as we are between exaltation
     and the abyss, waiting for words to rise
     in us like sun. All these years I've known you
     seem like a short moment, and that whole
     time you have been a cantankerous, sweet singer
     teasing the edge of some new vision—
     often short tempered except when shepherding
     in a metaphor to make the whole world shimmer
     with the thing that "herons know without
     the slightest hint of wind or wing." No matter
     how far you've traveled from that shore
     where herons priest, their lessons track you down.
     I read "24th Meditation" to my students again last week,
     and it made them hungry for good images
     and as wise as words can make one.
     Fred, bark at the crazy world as much
     as you must, but keep sending poems—
     I need their light to live by and your love
     of language rocking meaning out of the dark
     alleys at the edges of our lives to help me to survive.
     I hope you write another forty years
     at least, and at a hundred years to heaven,
     my letters will still find you
     singing startling images above the dirt.
     If not, we'll have to move our sparks
     into new wombs and just come back
     to this uncertain world where "all the shocks
     that flesh is heir to" give us too little grace
     and so many possibilities to rattle words

into sweet, clubfooted poems that can dance.

Love,
Gail

P.S. Stop smoking with Bukowski
on the phone. Good talk and old
memories are enough. I know
smoke is seductive, but it can reach
its hidden fingers into cells and work
such evil magic; at your age it's never
worth the risk you've taken over time.
Write soon, I need your letters,
the good news about publishing
and most of all the two or three new
poems, those stumbling revelations
that your haunted muses taunt you
to make mere human words refine.

Before Surgery for Endometrial Cancer, January, 2001

Waiting to give magic over to a drugged sleep
I would not choose, aware pain waits
like an unwelcome gift on the other side,
should I awake, I decide to dare to trust
a stranger, to go under the knife willingly
and take a chance at life— sweet life with all
its agony and beauty, its chance to love, its loss
hiding behind that uncertain door the future
uses to dare us to be brave. I try to prepare
myself to struggle through an inevitable fog
that will rob me of unbearable sensation,
create a hole in what I know, an emptiness
where organs have filled my interior world, where
cells divided in the dark and grew into a tumor
that will be examined and thrown away
with so much tender flesh that has been part
of me. I steel myself, plan, if I awake, to count
the days 'til I am in my own bed easing myself
into that private work that sprouts from the end
of my pen and teaches me what no drug can:
life is the act of feeling too many things breaking
like restless waves on the beach of each new day.

Sometimes

desire wakes like a prickle
on my tongue; I long
to taste the salt on a lover's
skin, to finger the damp region
that vibrates until a whole being
moans and turns and shivers
with unbearable pleasure. I long
to sink, to almost drown in the depths
of feeling, emotion washing over
me, wave after wave, drawing me
into an ocean where nothing
but sensation makes sense, and I
become the giver of impossible gifts
that somewhere another being wants.
But scarred by age and an insatiable
hunger, I no longer trust any creature
to lust for my touch, to roll over
and purr or murmur were I to stroke
soft skin or breathe sweet nothings
into the hollow of an ear. No longer
possessed with the beauty of my youth,
I do not dare rejection, won't propose
or wait among the stars to be the center
of some sad passion that might never be.
 Instead, I whisper, voice vibrating wind
against the smooth edges of a feather,
and know mere love is a feeling that can
expand like a ceremony to heal
the edges of a sad and lonely world.

Letter Poem for the Spirit of Martha Tapia, Too Early in Spring

Dear Martha,
    The day you died, darkness descended early.
Daylight savings was still six days away—
and living, I was left to weep, surrounded
by shadows, aware there would be no miracles
to ease me from a sorrow I had watched invade
my life as tumors in your body took your breath
away. The electric current that had coursed
through your brain withdrew, and your tender
hands became too still; loss filled me
with longing, and a million memories started
to stumble, haltingly, across my tongue.

Now, nineteen days later, I hunger for new stories,
the sound of your voice embroidering images
so magical the world came alive when you spoke.
Time will pass: already hyacinths along your walkway
fade, and my yard is a riot of tulips and daffodils
we do not share. The leaves of irises begin to swell
and soon bud stalks will stand tall; flowers we bought
together will bloom into a world where I must bear
a spring without you laughing in my garden as bees
brush their bellies on the fuzzy beards that mark the path
into that magic chamber that makes new seed possible.
How I miss you, your gentle love that made space for me
in a life full of grace. Even without your physical
presence, I know our love is a perennial,
though now I can not help but water it with salty tears.

Travel well, good soul—

                        Gail

Ceremony for Remembering
(Because we have lost Julie Bartow)

In that dark whistling moment
when the night bird calls one's name
and whispers to one about the death
of someone close and dear, when loss
comes like a thief stealing that sweet
electric thing that inhabits the skin
of someone one longs to touch, and leaves
one rocking in a sea of grief, one has little
choice but to embrace feeling and weep
at the cessation of so many sweet moments
that made life swell with joy. In such
circumstance, the act of being tough
would callous the soul, shut spirit out
and make one shrink from what is brave
and generous on earth. During the hours
when breath feels sharp inside the lungs
and tears come to sting one with salty precision,
until the tender hide feels stretched tight and too small
to contain a sorrow so expansive it haunts the margins
of the cells that vibrate against air. A human can feel
so hollow, each breath seems to swallow hope—
it is then that one grows to realize that memory
builds bridges from the edges of what feels
most empty, so even while we release what must go,
love lets us draw in like a breath that terrifying
grace that keeps some essence of what once was
forever alive in us

Trying to Make Sense
        (Upon the death of Margery Brown)

For months, I woke and cried for miracles,
whispered in every language I know,
addressed spirits that rule the stars,
invoked the giants who take pain away.
I prayed to unnamed forces that might
make tumors disappear. I tried to make
deals with angels, with dancing gods
and goddesses; I begged and begged
for spontaneous remission, for healing
that would slow the wild multiplication
of cells that overwhelm muscle walls, invade
organs and compromise the body's will
to be. I wished for a world where grace prevailed,
and the good did not die young. For more
than a year, I called out once or twice a day,
held good thoughts in my mind, refused to accept
that loss need be inevitable, that breath
and the wild electric pulse that feeds the brain
could leave my friend. It made no sense
that early death could rob the earth of her gift—
of her ability to spark others to take creative risks
and dream their own magic into being. But gods
are jealous and test us in our sweet desires;
being free of bodies, gods do not care about hands,
or hearts, or, eyes, or the lessons, that being human,
we learn fishing at the edges of infinity with finite senses.
So now I face this moment after my friend's
spirit has leapt like a simple wish to wash
agony away from a body no human had the wit
to cure, and I know that love can not be swept
away by this passing. A million memories bind us,
even as soul wings away from hollow flesh, and haunted
by mortality, I'm taught tenderness by heartless death.

Possibilities for Being Human

To Find a Tenderness

If I love, it is magic because the darkness
of it all surrounds me like a womb where infinite
possibilities are being born. There in the amniotic
sea where cells come together, then divide
over and over in some divine plan so mysterious
it can utterly transform the planet, new life
beats a steady pulse; the mind learns to haunt
a brain which grows in folds and hums
with the electric current that makes motion
inevitable. After a few months a curious
being swims down a tube tearing its way
into the air, sucks wind into lungs
and wails out a vision that shimmers
out of focus in the dancing light. Miraculous,
it blinks and waits while hands wipe
it dry, cut its last connection to the interior
world and with a quick stitch, define it
as separate and whole. At that moment the journey
out of loneliness begins in the arms of a mother
overwhelmed by feeling on an earth where nothing
is simple and need rattles the sense. Touch
soothes moments which contradict a solitude that drags
time across endless intervals of longing, making
a person cry out and reach across space
to find a tenderness that among all the names
will reach back and whisper one's own.

To Travel Generations

Sometimes dancing down the world, love overwhelms
one like a sweet shower of light making visible
lines from the tops of high trees to illuminate
a patch of ground and warm all the tiny growing
things that feed the soul's imagining. Some dark
form, hair cascading like a black river to the waist
will step graceful across a street littered
with memories and the remnants of an impossible
feast, will lift a foot past bones and the shards
of shell to haunt a hundred dreams where passion
turns and whispers a name. Moments blossom opening
with terrifying grace and senses tingle as brittle
as the music of deer hooves clacking on the ankles
of dancers who move around the drum to make
the whole world fertile. One's own breath, moving
past the tongue and over lips, fills moist space
with an incredible longing only touch will satiate.
In such moments, one realizes loneliness is irrelevant.
Risk becomes as inevitable as the rotation of seasons
or the movement of the wind. Every atom of one's being
vibrates charged with the electricity generated
by the infernal motion of too much feeling being born.
It is this force that fuels possibility, allows life,
that brief adventure, to travel generations under sun.

Finding a Way

In open country, the eye travels across
distance searching for landmarks in relation
to horizon, rests on stationary objects,
a bush, a tree, a swell of dirt
caused by wind blowing silt from the river
across centuries to make a rise in the landscape.
It is not as though earth is ever barren;
always, the lush grass bears seed to feed
the hungry bird or deer who in turn feeds
any carnivore quick enough to stop a life.
But in such a place, one needs to notice detail
to find one's way back to the waterhole, off
to the chokecherry grove, across to the next village
where love waits with all its mystery. Direction
whispers following the trail of the sun across
a wide sky leading one to face east in the morning,
west in the afternoon, knowing north is on one hand
or the other and south warms the opposite side
of the face on a good day. In such a world, one grows
to learn subtlety is the essential act of knowing
where one is and knowing how to find one's way.

Love wakes such strange sensitivities
between creatures, makes nuance
out of subtle movements that are imperceptible
to strangers who do not reach with feeling
across space. Concern can be born
from pain crossing like a cloud over
a good friend's face, casting a shadow
under the eyes as tiny muscles change the angle
of the brows so slightly that no mere acquaintance could
ever notice what causes a woman who cares
to reach across an electrically charged expanse
of air to touch another person whose gestures
she knows too well to ever ignore. Feeling
makes some things transparent like sunlight
swallowing a leaf, lighting its whole being,
revealing the magical web of veins that feed
the cells, revealing tiny scars made by insects
hungry to survive in this world where plants
transform the light to feed us all. One can look
at another person and see the whole being, light
humming in the cells, the little place where injury
stops energy, where impulse can no longer jump
across synapses, or where sensation creates static,
a flashing of signals that make tiny twitches
in the muscle of a cheek reacting to memory so sharp
response becomes inevitable. It is this gnawing
sensation, the million points of balance between joy
and agony that beg for recognition, that cause
a human who can not shut others out to suffer
this romance with awareness of the barely visible.

In Praise of Flesh

The touch of tongue to tongue, too intimate
to make a sense impression in the ear,
may wake desire that can haunt the wit,

but mouth is moist and dark, with definite
sharp edges that might make a cautious person fear
the touch of tongue to tongue. Too intimate!

Still, breath that caresses skin and tickles it,
that titillates nevre endings that are near,
may wake desire that can haunt the wit

until, aroused, taste learns lust for the exquisite
sauciness that teaches lovers to revere
the touch of tongue to tongue. Too intimate,

two, in an embrace, dare to dance with infinite
delight past that edge where any sigh they hear
may wake desire that can haunt the wit.

And so it is, flesh can draw in nimble spirit,
tempt synapses to move new beings as they appear,
so that the touch of tongue to tongue— too intimate—
will wake desire that can haunt the wit.

In those moments before dawn, when blue-gray edges
the horizon and so many things begin to hum
with expectation, when the night birds start
to rock themselves to sleep, the gentle breath
of the planet murmuring to them before the breeze
cleans its pipes out with the whistle of day, one
senses a shift. An eminent presence that makes
life possible stalks the distance, preparing
to snatch us from dreams into a world where possibility
wakes the voice, and the first day bird sings. The long
sorrow unravels into too many memories, and love
shimmers from mind, a mist rising over a warm expanse
of water to dance above the surface in a tingling cool
environment of air. Breath waits like a prayer,
barely audible, as it whispers mystery into being. When sun
finally rises, edging above the trees, over the backs
of sacred mountains and creates the blue mirage of sky,
the flute-like music of morning flows through beaks
and makes strange harmonies, notes winging against
the rhythm of the heartbeat as day becomes inevitable.
Suddenly, physical reality develops a million whirling
shadows that will shrink as morning lengthens, then move
in graceful dance concealing and revealing a million
miracles. Morning begins to stretch, to wake us
to our work, and in an instant we confront the endless
activity of defining our direction in relation
to complicated patterns that both nurture and destroy.

Meditation on the Edge of a Rainforest

On long gray days, when the mist is steady
and makes air seem to pulse in a constant beat
too quiet for the ear to apprehend, one feels
the plants expand as moisture swells their cells.
It is possible to imagine the moaning pleasure
of growth and birth as seeds burst their skins,
unroll roots and tiny stems that will stretch
and push the nurturing dirt while miraculous life
unfolds. It is this knowing below the threshold
of sensation that tickles the intuition and makes
the human mind awake to mystery. So much motion
takes place at speeds we cannot see; the purposeful
bursting of the calyx, the opening of petals
so that what one moment we recognize as bud,
the next day is flower attracting bees, who in love
with bright color and heady scent, buzz in bearing
pollen that leads to new seed. Often what we perceive
as death is the ripening that makes life possible.
Season follows season as earth tilts. Clouds and sun
do a complex dance so that water rises and falls.
What we know of all this activity has been
shaped by machines men invent to measure things
the naked eye can't see; curiosity outstrips
human limitations. So much we try to learn
is merely theoretical, a guess, a flimsy vision,
a metaphor that lets us hope we can puzzle out
life's meaning. Sitting in this limp drizzle,
it is startling to recognize the enormous
complexity that makes this moment possible.

To the Ghosts of Salmon

For generations, we have caught salmon
dressed in lovely flesh, skins shimmering
with scales, bellies iridescent as pearl
covering glorious coral-colored muscle
that quivers while fish shimmy upstream.
Only the strongest swim past our nets
and traps at the end of a remarkable
migration to make new life— to pass
on wisdom in simple cells, to make
eggs like small, translucent, orange jewels
grow fertile in tender gravel beds at the heads
of streams that hover in the body of memory
through years of travel in open ocean.
Grown, adults will swim, like their parents
miraculously, some to us, some past,
on their single journey home to spawn.

For generations, salmon have caught us,
filled us, enriched our lives, made the people
strong, have fed the eagles and the bears,
have haunted all our dreams and prayers,
their spirits awake in our imaginations;
we honor ghosts of salmon who even now
struggle to continue to make the circle
that supports our lives sacred and still whole.

Planetary Jazz
    (for Ornette Coleman)

Wind makes leaves reflecting sun shimmer,
makes light and shadow dance, creates intricate
patterns that are dizzying to one's sense
that repose is ever possible on this planet
caught up in mad motion. Even what seems rooted
is never really still; tranquility is illusion,
more emotion than reality, a reaction to shutting
out the narrow concerns of human invention
and sensation. In the world everything is rocking,
opening and closing, whirring, buzzing, wailing,
a disordered miracle waking us to the possibility
of vision, to time rising and setting, rotating
farther and closer near the sun. We wake to wilder
dreams, momentary nature, life always beginning,
always ending, the remains, rank and rotting, making
the planet fertile, the circle of things supporting
life whirling in this shambles that make life
possible. It is this breakdown, these teaming moments
moving past joy and sorrow that rock us in the cradle
of a universe we can barely come to know. What we
feel is mere reaction to infinity singing a soul.

Change of Seasons

Day after day, I must wake
to a life without roses, frost
reaching into my garden to curl
the tender leaves and make soft
petals drop away from stamens
lonely for pollen-covered bees
who could make spent flowers
swell like tiny apples, fruit
bearing seed to create mysterious
crossings born in a whispering earth
too subtle to need love to usher
in a new generation. Day after day,
I must wait as earth rotates
farther from, then closer to the sun,
through months too dark to warm
my heart, the beehives, my plants
which used to give off heady scents
and fill my transitory world with joy.

Trapped by Magic

In the place where dark and light meet,
comfort is always beside the point.
We negotiate with sensation that washes
over us like unruly weather and feel
the interminable prickle of hot and cold
etching a history on our skin. No hide
is thick enough to do more than screen
the inevitable pain that dances its bony
jig and waltzes so many we love away
into that ethereal reality where bodies
are superfluous and the will makes
its rumbling mark tracing lightning
across charged particles of sky. Caught
in the flesh, we explore miracles of touch,
knowing love makes us vulnerable to loss
as surely as it opens us to exquisite moments
where passion sweeps in and makes everything
possible. Then, in an instant of trance, spirit,
tempted by desire, enters that amniotic sack
where cells divide, and trapped by magic,
grows complex so that even amid
all this dying, creation continues.

Days

There are days when grace is as simple
as the whisper of narrow leaves moving
in the breeze; the fragrance of sweetgrass
soothes the mind; then smell becomes
a passageway opening into all that is
wholly beautiful and wakes memory
of ceremony dancing with as much spirit
as bright feathered birds leaping into wind.

There are days when grace is as melancholy
as owls singing a soul away; then dark
magic blooms in the fire releasing flesh
from all the pain and limitation of being
human. The rind sloughs off and fertilizes
Earth, that fast moving woman who takes
what rots into herself to make new life;
spirit escapes; tingles naked in the shocking air.

There are days when grace refuses to wake,
and longing fills the tunnels of rich blood
pulsing from dark chambers sequestered
in the ribcage out of sight, pumping
bright waves that feed the lonely cells
'til they remember how to invoke the sacred
names that call forth song. Then we sing
and grace comes around to touch our tongues.

29105006R20054

Made in the USA
Charleston, SC
02 May 2014